Piercing the Veil

poems by

Maryam Hand

Finishing Line Press
Georgetown, Kentucky

Piercing the Veil

ACKNOWLEDGMENTS

The following poems have been previously published:

"Cheating the Salamander" - published in *Maryam Hand's Poetry in Relation to Sufi Teachings and to the Tradition of Sufi Authorship,* Bettaieb, Rym, Ph.D., Drew University.
"Heart Child" - published in *Moon Journal,* and *Maryam Hand's Poetry in Relation to Sufi Teachings and to the Tradition of Sufi Authorship,* Bettaieb, Rym, Ph.D., Drew University.
"My Complicated Father"- published in *Calliope,* 14th Annual Anthology of *Women Who Write,* and second place winner in their 2007 International Poetry Contest.
"Spearchucka" - published in *Moon Journal* and *Maryam Hand's Poetry in Relation to Sufi Teachings and to the Tradition of Sufi Authorship,* Bettaieb, Rym, Ph.D., Drew University.

Publisher: Leah Maines

Editor: Christen Kincaid

Cover Art: Rachel Mauser

Author Photo: Joshua Mauser

Cover Design: Elizabeth Maines

Printed in the USA on acid-free paper.
Order online: www.finishinglinepress.com
                    also available on amazon.com

Author inquiries and mail orders:
Finishing Line Press
P. O. Box 1626
Georgetown, Kentucky 40324
U. S. A.

Table of Contents

To my parents, Paul and Gloria Hand, for bringing me into this world and raising me with love.

To my children: Nathan, Rachel, Joshua, and David for their undying love, support and belief in me over the years.

To my beloved husband, Isa, for loving me with a heart as vast as the ocean and for receiving all the love I have to give, for accompanying me on this life journey towards wholeness and for being the ground supporting, encouraging and sometimes insuring that I honor my calling.

To my beloved spiritual guide, Sidi, for plucking me out of the abyss of darkness and pain and guiding me ever so gently and patiently to the Light. There are no words to adequately express my gratitude.

Preface

In the Name of God, the Most Merciful, the Most Compassionate

January 1, 2016

Last night, I welcomed the New Year in the same way as I have for the past twenty something years. I spent a substantial part of the night in prayer: reflecting with gratitude on all the good that has come into my life, asking for forgiveness for the mistakes I have made, praying for guidance, setting my spiritual and earthly intentions for the coming year, and opening a space to commune with My Beloved. I have been, for as long as I can remember, one who has found happiness and peace in those exquisite moments of loving intimacy with "The One," and someone who also has found misery, restlessness and depression in long periods of disconnection and veiling. Last night, the wondrous gift of the sweetest intimacy, something that I do not take for granted and am sure comes through grace, rather than as a result of personal accomplishment, held a teaching for me. As the light poured into my grateful vessel, I wondered if perhaps, when enough of the veils are pierced, when enough of the resistance has washed away, when we say yes to the love and mercy more than we say no, perhaps then we can more easily open the door of our heart to our Beloved's generous outpouring and find elusive heavenly peace here, on this planet.

I hope and pray this book finds its way into the hands, hearts and souls of those who are searching for inner peace, for a deeper meaning to life, for a greater Reality than that which meets the eye, and for love, healing and wholeness. When the time is right and the soul is yearning, even a momentary glimpse through the veil and the accompanying "taste" can be enough to bring hope to a restless soul and open the way to heal a heart bereft of "The Beloved." I pray these poems give the reader a glimpse of something worth searching for.

In peace,
Maryam Hand

Spearchucka

I

"Spearchucka," the boys yell
as I near the school.
A cluster of heads lean out
from the second story window,
shout to me with a mixture of teasing
and admiration.

I am carrying my javelin—
smooth, silvery metal
cool in my hand.
I feel like a warrior.

I wait all day to hear the dismissal bell
announce my freedom
then practice my throw for hours
alone
in the big field behind the school.

II

In my sleep at night,
I dream about perfect flight.
The weight of the sleek spear in my hand,
the pull on my shoulder as my arm
extends back, straight elbowed.
I can just see the silver point
in peripheral vision.

I look up,
focus,
aim at an imaginary
luminous smoke ring
up in the blue sky.

Then comes the precisely measured, all out sprint,
the lightning-quick torque,
squaring of shoulders and finally,

explosive release.

And my javelin's propelled
toward heaven's door
as if it were my own soul.

III

When a throw comes together perfectly,
time pauses.
Motion slows surreally.
I watch my beauty soar.

Arcing silver gleams,
dazzles light,
then lands, tip burrowing into the earth
far, far across the field.
Home again.

IV

Last night I dreamed
I found my high school javelin,
held its battered body
across my palm,
cocked my middle-aged arm
ready to launch.

But always
something was wrong:
the wind
or people in my throwing range.
Then I couldn't find the
perfect balancing point,
so critical.
Then I lost the javelin.

I woke bereft,
yearning—
that perfect throw
the silver soul
flying precisely
to its destination home.

Full Moon

Years ago,
our land bordering,
we—
mystics savoring solitude,
separately thread our way
through silent, silvery woods washed
in midnight moon.

Serendipity laughs
or perhaps, soul lights beckon.
Our startled shadows mingle
far from city lights.

> Sometimes
> when alone
> love caresses my heart.
> Being human
> as well as spirit
> I long for a person to love;
> I imagine soft or hard kisses.

By moon's bright guidance, we tread
past looming ancient oaks
silhouetted in ghostly light,
past my composting toilet outhouse—
monument of salvaged cedar shakes,
with its hand painted purple door embossed with
red heart.

> It's strange, having been
> alone so long
> only to have love
> rise up out of its sleeping bed,
> unexpectedly,
> and hurry to burn me.
> I wonder, "Who sends this love?"
> Love replies, "I do."

We pass a listing barn,
the chill night air, crisp.
A Great Horned Owl rustles,
folds itself
into the willowy native grass
with deadly intention.
The owl's wings
beat laboriously upward,
weighted
against the shimmering moon glow.

We find,
trace the gravel road.
Turn right
toward his hand built cabin,
the promised ginger tea,
the oil-lamp's rosy
expectant glow.

I surrender to this invisible
love breathed into my
throbbing heart
as I lie here alone,
in solitary light.
Full moon shining
through my bedroom window.

My Complicated Father

Your ego,
delicate,
is as fragile as the hand-blown hummingbird
cradled gently in my palm.
My child hand trembles in its effort
to protect glass wings
that threaten to shatter.

I learn to reach out to you
tentatively
the way a child stretches out a tiny hand
offers sugar cubes to a skittish horse
in supplication
innocently, nervously
never knowing if the sweet offering will be accepted
or if ears will lie back
and teeth bare.

Your moods, as unpredictable and dark
as storm clouds
orchestrate
our gyrations and prostrations
until I grow weary of this dance
and search for a different God.

Until I grow angry
put on blinders
plug my ears and crash into delicate china
shatter any peace that my sensitive
sister can find.
I have to survive.

Your unknowable hiding heart
once sang love poems to your beloved,
my mother.
Last night, my own hair gray,
I read the yellowed pages of your testimony—

could scarcely recognize you
beneath the crusty barnacles that now cover
like they protect the tender belly of an old whale.
Your love tainted by persistent angst,
like one who tosses with a fever
like one who has battled demons.

And still, you are more gentle with her
than I have ever seen you.
Your love for her is true.

Now, I watch the patterns
play like sunlight on water.
Iridescent, with a lightness
that shatters tombs.
Your silver white dignity
still fraught with lingering shadows
does not imprison me.
I cradle lovingly in my palm
the glass hummingbird of my own fragile ego.

Piercing the Veil

Snow flurries swirl like sufi dervishes
against a dark canvas
of monotony.
One headlight fixes on the looming buck; my wandering mind
lurches to full alert.
A palpable presence enters my hands;
guides the wheel as though slicing
through a space the width of a date hair.
Tires whine and stutter along the shoulder ridges;
sound like sirens screaming.
We rush past the beast. I imagine
the pressurized whooshing air pushing
against his hindquarters, parting his coarse hair
like a tidal wave.
Then, the definitive moment,
the Previa careens, leans—
as though it will leap over the guardrail and pursue
its own finality.
But the presence guides precisely and the Hands
of Divine Intention smooth our course.
An open ended fragment of timelessness
collapses into but a moment in my awareness.
I glance at the ashen face of my oldest son;
catch the comprehension
frozen in his expression—
How we brushed
Death
while three innocents slumbered in the backseat.

The next day I open the newspaper:
Previa.... 4 kids....swerved to avoid a deer.....tumbled over the
guardrail... one child died.

Poverty

1.
Last night, I sat in the absence of light
where my heart used to be
waiting for God to strike
a frail match.

I strain
in thin wavering light
to glimpse
past shadows.

2.
Later, I type, "Two Sister Kitties Free
to a Good Home" and hit "send."
I do not write about the emptiness.

My majestic husky
sniffs his new Norbourne Estates
backyard. Fenced, clean
white people play being rich.
The neighbor, wound so tight,
raps angrily on the door and screams
about my car parked on the street
after seven —against the ordinance
of the wealthy. I try to tell his apoplectic
face that I just want to see
my kids but he can't hear me.

At least my boys have their dog
and their balding dad when he comes home
from another long day examining feet
and plays solitaire on the computer.

3.
My clothes—the ones I couldn't take with me,
some blankets, a sewing machine, books,
the hand painted old table I couldn't bear to sell,
live in a friend's basement.
I live elsewhere,
at house number three,
the third in five months,
in a room with a mattress on the floor,
two plastic tubs of clothes and
treasured books:
Music of the Soul, The Sufi Realities.
My computer on the collapsible table
faces the window. I gaze
past the dead flies squashed on the underside
of the old broken blind
to the three bright red cardinals
chorusing through the air
to the house where the teenage boys hang out
instead of going to school
and steal, instead of working
to pay for their drugs.

4.
I used to live in the East End
in a pretty pale yellow house
with cats curled up
under a brightly painted yellow sun
rising on the vaulted living room wall,
with bookcases
full of treasured books:
The Secret of the Love of God, Wisdom for the Devoted,
a fenced yard for my dogs,
a fireplace for my kids to roast marshmallows
stuffed with chocolate chips
and a garden full of fruit trees,
forsythias,
and bright little redbirds.

5.
I sit,
in the absence of life
with my kids
and search the place
where my heart used to be.

The Meeting of Adam and Eve

Her shy lids unveil
eyes like limpid pools.
He gazes, enters naked.
Like sugar, he dissolves.
Her soft waters of light
receive him.
Immersed in her essence
he remembers himself.

His eyes reflect,
like clear deep pools
his remembrance.
She drinks
in a formless world where
light mingles with light
in perfect unity.
She is home.

Heart Child

Four months pregnant
and suddenly
I am tiny, inside the womb
watching my baby boy.
I name him my
"Heart Child."

Eighteen months old,
eating lunch in his high chair,
I gaze into large
green-brown eyes.
All time stops
and I fall,
fall
into his soul.

Four years old,
sitting in a sleeping bag
poised
at the top of the stairs,
he turns and smiles at me,
waves, and instructs,
"Say good-bye to your 'Heart Child!'"
I am astonished.
I never called him by that name out loud.
He zips down the stairs,
laughing.
"How did you know you are my Heart Child?"
"I just know."

They are all beloved to me, my children.
They are all unique and special.
But he stands a little taller within himself,
fifteen years old,
knowing that
he,
he is called,
"Heart Child."

The Value of Life

Dragging that cedar by one small branch through dark woods I own,
a Screech Owl flushes, startles last night's dreams—the sharply put,
watch your step!

I disregard the omen, slide the cedar over a tree growing sideways
across my path
until my ambling thoughts are interrupted with a snap and a crack of
the dislocating branch against my jaw and the violent counter descent
of the cedar into the soft of my belly.

My huskies watch while pain swallows me like a toad swallows a fly
and spirit wrenches from its shivering body-temple, flies higher and
higher, almost free.

Regret washes over what is left of me. Reaching back with desperate
fingers,
I fight the current that wants to drag me away. Then with one
horrendous effort
I am on my back again, fading in and out of consciousness.

It is dark when I awake to a voice. *Stay in this life for your body is God's
and you are His mirror.*

The Seventh Morning of the Women's Artist Retreat

On black lacquered lawn chair, before breakfast
inspiration incubates in silence.
I watch: glossy green bug washes its crusty face,
red-headed fly grooms its legs,
horsefly plunks itself against the patio door, falls,
spins on its back like a break dancer
then shakes its head and flies away, complaining.

The lawnmower drones like a gnat
far across the field on the other side of the farmhouse.
Soon lawnmower guy approaches my quiet zone,
circles the tree too close to me.
Distant summer drone turned roaring monster—
devouring solitude. The smell of gas mingles with
the fragrance of massive verdant decapitation.

Edgy, I debate pulling my bare feet down from their table top perch
and gathering my books, prayer beads, pen
but curious, I spy. He is like a storm
spinning around trees, head down, blue baseball cap pulled low,
thin white tee-shirt, stuck to his sweaty back,
knocked knees, pressed together
spinning around trees, spinning around trees
then, at last, droning away.

I take a full in-breath, let out an audible sigh, uncurl my toes
and will my shoulders to drop two inches.
But he's soon back, weaving a chaotic pattern in the grass
and spinning around trees.
My patience, rocks, then pops
like the top of my mother's pressure cooker.

Muttering, I retreat—
defeated, to the kitchen.

1968 in Palestine

Refugees walk while clear shimmering heat rises in waves.
His little mouth feels like stuffed cotton and she, in whose arms
is his only home, wets her finger in her own mouth,
lets him suck on the meager moisture,
comforts him with her heart,
hides her tears
supports his innocence.

2005 in America,
the phone rings.
He scrambles to sell his laptop,
to cross an ocean of grief
to sit with her.
She smiles, kisses him,
remembers fleeing the village
his boy hand in hers,
their unquenchable thirst
for home.
Her mind runs the patterns of her life
through wrinkled, work-worn hands,
memories that move in air, imagining the
knitting, the embroidering, and the
gliding over prayer beads
until she quiets,
returns to her True Home.

2009
Perhaps it was the familiar
Middle Eastern food.
He sits across from me,
speaks of the journey,
tries to hide the storm in his heart.
His eyes reach back through the years.
He was five and her arms were his only home.

The Wedding

The crystal brimming with cool wine
And the wine imbibed.

The sweet white cake offered
And the eager, waiting mouth.

The breath that mingles in the kiss.

The light that spills from expressive eyes,
And the yearning to merge as One.

The wineglass crushed underfoot.

The blessed union.

Dawn Prayer

In inky light,
I drag myself from warm cocoon
then dash through nipping air.
My feet recoil on stinging tile.

At the porcelain sink,
I splash water on cringing,
goose fleshed skin
too cold to wait
for warmth to flow
through crusty iron pipes.

I pull on warm wool socks,
wrap the moss green shawl tightly
around my contracted vessel
and cover my head
with a soft flowing scarf.

I pause,
brain and body numb
while dreams snatched
from interrupted sleep
flash across an inner screen,
search for meaning,
for a place to settle,
and settle roughly.

Then, the dawn bird high
in the bush begins to sing.
Sweet bird. She greets the first light
of this new day. I smile,
forgetting my cold misery,
to hear her praising God.
Her whole body, like her voice,
quivers with love.

Together, we raise our voices.

Labyrinth

Entering the spiral grass path,
I yield to the prescription,
"drop the self-direction."
Mystery opens her gates.

Journeying across unseen borders
I hear myself sing *Your Name*
as if from a distant place,
lost in the breath as it flows,
no longer aware of moving feet,
of fingers sliding over prayer beads
or of the joining
with You.

Your unseen hand guides
until, shocked, I return to my self
standing in the *Center*.

My mind struggles to understand
this foreign territory—

Time folded up
and there was only *You.*

Naked

His barnacled heart
like a warrior's shield,
deflects poisonous arrows
and sweet intimacy—both
until he is starved
for her delicate touch.

Her subtle breezes caress
his crusty walls of hard
earned protection.
Deep within his center
he secretly weeps.

She whispers through
the compressed sediment
of pain over time
and warms his fossilized tears
until they spill openly,

until they wash his fortressed heart.
She enters, touches his
tender flesh with her warm breath,
fans his fragile flame
until veils are ignited,

until he stands
naked before her.

Cheating the Salamander

Analyzing poetry,
with conversation bordering on the absurd.
Stifled chuckles tickle my solar plexus.
Are we cheating the salamander?

White salamander,
soul unblemished,
traveler from Pre-Eternity
arrives here at the outer reaches of everything.
Arrives and is lost.
Knowing, forgetting and knowing again.

Veils amorphously settle around the heart
obscuring its brilliant purity
even to itself,
until it is loved back into True Existence
through mystical moments of grace.

Is this just a cheap shot from some sadistic God?
Unwrap the gauze-covered wound
and gaze upon its ugly brokenness with love, if you can.
Unwrap the gift.
Laugh through the paradox
and find the key to open the door to the Light that is already there.

Enter the brightly lit tavern
and sip chalices of wine.
Suddenly your cheeks are aching from grinning
and silenced chuckles roll out uncontained.
Chalices tipping;
wine spilling everywhere.
And you! rolling on the floor,
gasping for breath through giggles.

Nothing looks the same anymore.
What Reality is this?
And how did it change?
The last thing I remember before taking that drink,
was that we were worried about cheating the salamander.

Paw Paw Tree

I notice a young paw paw tree,
growing under the old crab apple
by the brown slat fence.
Her drooping green leaves
mottled with scabby brown spots
speak of a harsh spring freeze,
the months of summer drought,
of how she drew to the center
all her strength
and waited for rain.

Now, a charging charcoal sky
promises change.
I think of planting
a companion tree
deep in the clay,
to drink the rain,
to grow strong roots that reach,
intertwine like lover's fingers,
and bear fruit.

I remember my dream:
We dance in perfect synchronicity.
His essence lingers
long after the sun has grown yellow and strong.

The Prophet

Deep in my rose garden, we meet.
He has waited, being a jealous lover,
until I keen for him alone.
His eyes pour love into my awe-crumbled, hungry heart.
His effulgent face dazzles like sun diamonds on virgin snow—
translucent skin, a shifting mirage in the dancing light,
a body that casts no shadow.

Bare Love

An icy rain peppers against the tin roof
hurls against the dark loft window, then pearls
and falls away.
My body, scooped perfectly by yours,
eager. The tension
of wild electrons whirring in my heart
contrasts with the lulling radiant warmth
of your skin.

Your chest rises and falls,
rises and falls more deeply and I realize
I will not kiss you this night.

The ache in my heart
surges like a tidal force,
cries out for connection
like a baby in the night,
like a child never held.
I want to run from the rising emptiness,
but you stir, murmur, "stay in my arms,"
before you drift away again
on a cloud of spirit.

"*Oh Beloved,*" I groan, from an aching pit.

Bare love rushes to enter my rusty chamber,
fills my heart a warm pink
while your chest rises and falls,
rises and falls.

Heartquake

After the heartquake
lava flows and burns inside my breast.
I call *Your Name*
while tumbling through the aftershocks.

I use *Your Name* as if to stomp out burning embers.
But this time
You do not work that way.

You send *Your Mercy* like the rain.

Laila

Far beneath your full faced, glorious moon,
lovers search interior fields to catch the scent of roses.
I come to *You* dressed in bridal veils.
You wrap me inside your woolen cloak, close
to your heart and cover my shyness.
I open to your secret. Your white fire purifies
my veils of separation; the door of your heart
opens a wide gateway.
You carry me to meadows of precious ripe dates.
We taste, break the long fast, giddy,
now veiled in Light, on this holy night of Laila.

The Seer

On a red, dusty road
outside the holy city
he walks with purpose,
as though to meet someone.
His simple gray djellaba,
the white cloth wrapped around his head,
the thonged sandals,
and the olive wood prayer beads that hang,
half in and half out of his pocket
stir in me both a curiosity and an aching, longing
though I do not know why.
He slows and I can see into green-gray eyes,
as unfathomable as an ancient sea.
I feel my heart rise up, lean towards him.
He searches my face
and satisfied, deepens his gaze
as though he can pierce the smoke veils of my shame
to lock his sight on a dazzling diamond
buried in the garden of my heart.
He bows his head, pulls the olive wood beads from his pocket,
places them in my hand
and turns to retrace his steps.

Later, alone under the courtyard palm,
my fingers sliding over the olive wood gift,
I travel the newly opened territory,
send my breath on a journey,
this time not stopping with veils
that shimmer like mirages in hot sand.
I sense my hidden jewel
and feel a soft portal open
to a warm and ancient sea inside myself.

Veils

The first day of school,
her wandering right eye refuses
to settle behind new light blue,
cat eye glasses.
The ophthalmologist's patch on the left eye,
the in toeing foot,
the turtle way she retracts her head between her shoulders
belies a five year old's innocence
makes me want to pin down that restless eye,
and ask her soul to speak.

That night, as dream fragments
fly in and out on misty clouds,
I hear her wise soul say,
it's like this:
the drama ends,
velvet curtains close across the stage, in layers,
lights go out,
memories sink like rocks in murky seas
until even the sound of their sinking
ceases.

Thirty years pass.
Reverberations ripple,
An invisible quaking shakes deep seas,
spews rocks upward
towards the sky,
towards the light.
Memories too painful;
she wants to die.
Back in that room
the curtains part.

And in a dream
tender hands
wipe at the veils
around her eye.

Additional Acknowledgements

I would like to acknowledge The One, The Beloved, The Intimate Friend, The Guide, The Giver of Life, The One Who Moves Me, The One Who Inspires Me, and The One in Whose Service I Hope to Be. I would also like to acknowledge and express my gratitude to the many people who have been part of the tapestry of my spiritual journey and therefore, my writing. Some of these people have made life changing contributions; some have been instrumental in my growth as a poet, and some have facilitated the process of bringing my poetry to light. Thank you One and All.

I must particularly single out Mary Ber, editor of *Moon Journal,* for her expert mentoring and compassionate support. Mary recognized my strengths as a spiritual seeker and writer and helped me develop as a poet while gently holding my heart during a very painful period in my life. She ultimately pointed me towards the Finishing Line Press, "New Women's Voices Competition."

Michael Jackman, head of the Louisville Writers Workshop Project, is an appreciated friend and was an excellent mentor during my writing years in Louisville.

Jamila Davies is a good friend and appreciated professional companion. Her "Writing from the Heart" workshops have been instrumental in validating and honoring the importance of writing in my life as a tool for self- expression, spiritual and personal growth.

I would like to thank Rym Bettaieb for using my poetry as the central feature in her Ph.D. dissertation. In doing so she opened a door for my poetry to enter the world and gave me the encouragement I needed to follow my muse. My poetry would still be in a file cabinet had she not walked into my life.

At the organizational level, I would like to acknowledge *The Kentucky Foundation for Women* and The KFW's Hopscotch House. Several of the poems in this book were written while attending an artist residency there. I would also like to mention and thank the Kentucky non-profit, *Women Who Write*, for their support, encouragement and education of women writers.

Finally, I would like to thank Leah Maines and Finishing Line Press for their commitment to women through the annual "New Women's Voices Competition." I owe the publication of this book to them.

Maryam Hand is a spiritual seeker, poet, and mother of four grown children. She was awarded Semi-Finalist in the 2015 Finishing Line Press, "New Women's Voices Series Chapbook Competition," for her latest poetry collection entitled, "Piercing the Veil."

Maryam's first manuscript, "The Garden in the Fire: A Spiritual Journey through Poetry," was published in 2013 as a Ph.D. dissertation by Rym Bettaieb, Ph.D., entitled, "Maryam Hand's Poetry in Relation to Sufi Teachings and to the Tradition of Sufi Authorship." Her poem, "My Complicated Father," earned second place in the "Women Who Write," 2007 International Poetry Contest and was subsequently published in their Anthology, *Calliope*. Several of Maryam's poems have appeared in *Moon Journal*. During her years spent in Kentucky, she was awarded several Artist Residencies at Hopscotch House in Louisville.

Maryam moved to rural Pennsylvania in 2009 both to enjoy and support a growing community of spiritually like-minded people. Here she met and married her beloved husband. In addition to writing, "Piercing the Veil," she has managed and emceed several heart centered music/poetry festivals for her community and organizes spiritual music/poetry coffeehouses both locally and in various parts of the country.

www.ingramcontent.com/pod-product-compliance
Lightning Source LLC
LaVergne TN
LVHW041328080426
835513LV00008B/628